# Me and Mine

# Me and Mine

## A SELF-DISCOVERY JOURNAL

**SIRIUS**
This edition published in 2025 by Sirius Publishing, a division of
Arcturus Publishing Limited,
26/27 Bickels Yard, 151–153 Bermondsey Street,
London SE1 3HA

Copyright © Arcturus Holdings Limited

All rights reserved. No part of this publication may be reproduced, stored
in a retrieval system, or transmitted, in any form or by any means,
electronic, mechanical, photocopying, recording or otherwise, without
prior written permission in accordance with the provisions of the
Copyright Act 1956 (as amended). Any person or persons who do any
unauthorised act in relation to this publication may be liable to criminal
prosecution and civil claims for damages.

All illustrations courtesy of Shutterstock

ISBN: 978-1-3988-5719-3
AD012274NT

Printed in China

We cannot choose our external circumstances, but we can always choose how we respond to them.

EPICTETUS

# Tranquil Reflections

Welcome to a book that is all about you! Here you are the star of the show, the leading actor on the stage of your life. One of the most transformative aspects of psychotherapy and psychology is that of self-awareness. Many people go through life with little to no self-awareness whatsoever, yet it makes sense that to live your best life, you need to know what it is that makes you tick. What riles you, what beguiles you? You need to understand where your triggers come from so that you can minimize their impact. You need to know what your unique gifts and talents are so that you can make the most of them. Most of all, you need to understand yourself at a deeper level in order to overcome challenges and make progress in your life.

This journal will act as a magic mirror of tranquil reflections, one that gives you the chance to reflect upon yourself, exploring your likes, dislikes, moods, struggles, joys and relationships. It can lead you step-by-step, and day-by-day, into a deeper understanding of who you are and why you do the things you do. The gentle Power Insights contained within these pages will guide you to your inner self, allowing you to reflect upon your past, present and future. This isn't a tool for addressing deep personal trauma, but a light-hearted exploration of your personality. By responding to the insights contained within these pages you are participating in a creative form of self-care and self-discovery.

Writing things down can help you to make connections and correlations you might otherwise miss. When your heart, head and hand

work together to respond to these journal insights, it triggers a response from your subconscious mind. You are in effect communicating with your higher self – a super-conscious, wise part of yourself – thereby excavating the deeper meaning of what it means to be you. Working on yourself in this way can help you to improve your self-esteem, confidence and relationships. All you have to do is write!

Try to think of yourself as a magical *wordsmith* – what you write, you create, through the alchemical magic of your pen. Make your responses to these journal insights as full and expansive as possible, focusing on just one or two insights at a time, in order to get the best results. Feel free to revisit the insights that resonate with you the most or which you feel most excited about. Above all, remember that it is a collaboration and a conversation between you and your higher self. When your higher self speaks, you will need to play your part in the process by taking positive action on those insights and suggestions.

Are you ready to become more in tune with yourself? If so, then it's time to pick up your magical pen and write your tranquil reflections into reality. Good luck and from one wordsmith to another, may your heart beat with happiness, peace and joy because self-knowledge is the greatest power of all.

Serene Blessings,
Jacqueline Bruce

# The Insights

*First say to yourself what you would be and then do what you have to do to become it.*

— EPICTETUS

# Power Insight One

## In The Beginning There Was YOU!

You are your only constant companion through life. You were there in the womb, you were there at your birth and you will be there at the end when you return to Spirit. You are the only person who is 100% guaranteed to be there for you consistently, through the good times and the bad. The relationship you have with yourself, therefore, is perhaps the most precious one of all.

*I always think of myself as being…*

*One of the main things I really like about myself is…*

*because...*

*I identify as someone who…*

*One of the ways I can show up for myself each day is to…*

*I support myself by…*

*If I had to describe myself as an object/food/animal I would say I was...*

*I am ruled by my…*

*because…*

*If I could change one thing about myself it would be…*

*because…*

# Power Insight Two

## Your Inner Child

The child you used to be is still an important aspect of your personality. In fact, chances are that your inner child still has an influence on all your decisions and the life you lead today. Acknowledging and nurturing your inner child can help you to enjoy life more and become more playful, while self-parenting a wounded inner child can be very healing indeed.

*When I was a child I would spend hours…*

*because it made me feel…*

*As a child I found it easy/difficult to make friends because…*

*My greatest childhood ambition was to…*

*and I can achieve that goal in adulthood by…*

*Playtime means…*

*and I can become more playful by…*

*Some routines from my childhood that I enjoyed include…*

*and I can incorporate them into my daily life in the following ways…*

*Some of the ways in which I can parent and nurture myself are…*

*When I do this or this happens…*
*I know that my inner child is trying to communicate with me…*

*so I will…*

*My inner child was wounded when…*

*I can help to heal this old wound by…*

*Something that frightened me as a child was…*

*and I can face/let go of this fear by…*

*As a child I always felt safe when…*

*and I can recreate this sense of safety by…*

# Power Insight Three

## Seasons Change

One of the most obvious signs of the passage of time lies in the changing seasons. What do the seasons mean to you? Do you honour the transitions from one season to the next, or do they pass you by without you really noticing them? Has the way in which you view the seasons of the year changed over time?

*As a child my most enjoyable season was…*

*because…*

*As an adult my most enjoyable season is…*

*because...*

*Some of the family traditions we had each season were…*

*Some new seasonal traditions I would like to create are…*

*Back to school season still makes me feel…*

*I love to spend my summer holidays…*

*because...*

*My ideal thing to do in my free time is…*

*because it makes me feel…*

*Christmas makes me want to…*

*A bonfire reminds me of…*

*I can bring the seasons into my life by…*

*If I were a season, I would be…*

*because...*

# Power Insight Four

## Your Relationships

How well you know yourself will determine how well you relate to others. If you find it difficult to talk to new people, it could be a remnant of old childhood insecurity. On the other hand, if you find yourself in the midst of one altercation after another, you might have some unresolved anger you need to express in a healthier way!

*My main caregiver as a child was…*

*and their personality traits were…*

*In my current life someone who reminds of this person is…*

*and our relationship is very…*

*Someone close that I didn't get along with as a child was…*

*Their traits were…and they made me feel…*

*In my current life, someone who reminds me of this person is…*

*and our relationship is very…*

*A person from my past that I was afraid/distrustful of is…*

*and ...reminds me of them.*

*My closest friend is…*

*and we get on because…*

*Someone I really admire is…*

*and I admire them because…*

*Someone I wish I was more like is…*

*because...*

*Authority figures always make me feel…*

*My boss is…*

*My spouse/partner makes me feel…*

*I get angry with people when they…*

*and I can work on this by…*

*I know I am getting angry/upset when…*

*and I can express it in a healthy way by…*

*I communicate best when…*

*Someone I can always talk to is…*

*Someone I find it hard to open up to is…*

*because...*

# Power Insight Five

## Your Ambitions and Hobbies

Having a hobby to work on or an ambition to strive for gives you a sense of purpose and direction in life. Whether you want to run a marathon, you're aiming for a promotion at work, you want to write a book, or something else, having something to aim for can keep you in a positive frame of mind and ensures that your life is progressing.

*I've always had a talent for…*

*I use this talent whenever I…*

*I would like to nurture it by…*

*A skill I would like to have is…*

*and I could acquire it by…*

*If I could do any job at all it would be...*

*The highest position I can see myself achieving is…*

*because...*

*If I tell myself...*

*then I could…*

*The limitations that surround me include…*

*I could break through these limitations by…*

*The possibilities that surround me are…*

*I could embrace and achieve these possibilities by…*

*I know that luck is on my side because…*

*My greatest achievement to date is…*

*and I can take the next step by…*

# Power Insight Six

## Your Emotional Intelligence

Understanding your emotions is a key skill because it means that they won't catch you off guard. If you recognize the signs that you are becoming overwhelmed or angry or upset, then you can take steps to control those emotions rather than letting the emotion control you. Likewise, if you track your day-to-day mood, you are more likely to spot patterns and correlations which you can then address.

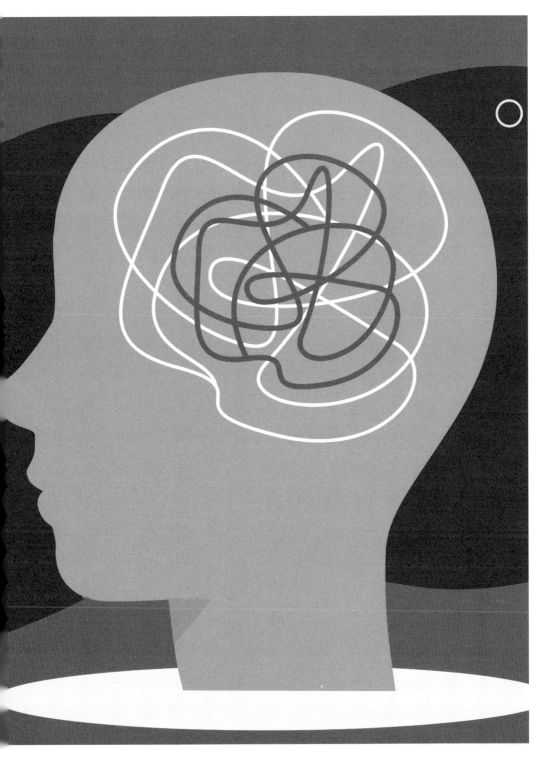

*How do I feel today, right now and where does this emotion come from?*

*What can I do to get more/less of this emotional state?*

*Where can I feel love in my body?*

*Where can I feel anger in my body?*

*Where can I feel fear in my body?*

*When was the last time I felt envy?*
*Who or what was I envious of and do I still feel this way?*

*What can I do to manage that emotion when it comes up again?*

*What are the signs that I am losing my temper?*

*How will I address this in future – walk away, work out, something else?*

*What triggers me the most and where did this trigger come from?*

*How can I deal with that issue?*

*When was the last time I felt loved and loving?*

*Who was I with, what was I doing?*

*When was the last time I felt safe?*

*Why?*

*What can I do to nurture this feeling of safety?*

*What makes me feel like I'm in control?*

*Do I have to be in control of everything and everyone, or am I happy to be led by others occasionally?*

*Am I a leader or a follower, or both and why?*

*How can I communicate better with others?*

*How can I best express myself?*

*What or who makes me laugh out loud?*

*How can I get more laughter in my life?*

# Lists of Note

*Who do I want to see more of in my life?*

- 
- 
- 
- 
- 
- 
- 
- 
- 
- 
- 
-

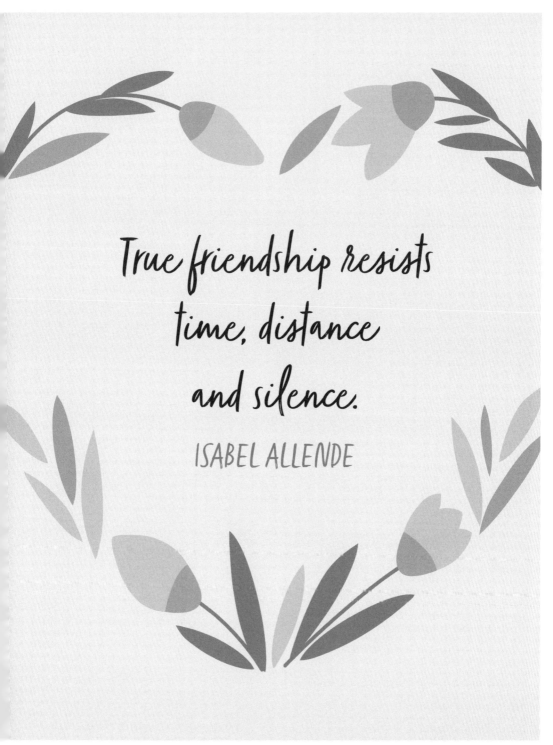

*Where in the world do I want to visit?*

- 
- 
- 
- 
- 
- 
- 
- 
- 
- 
- 
-

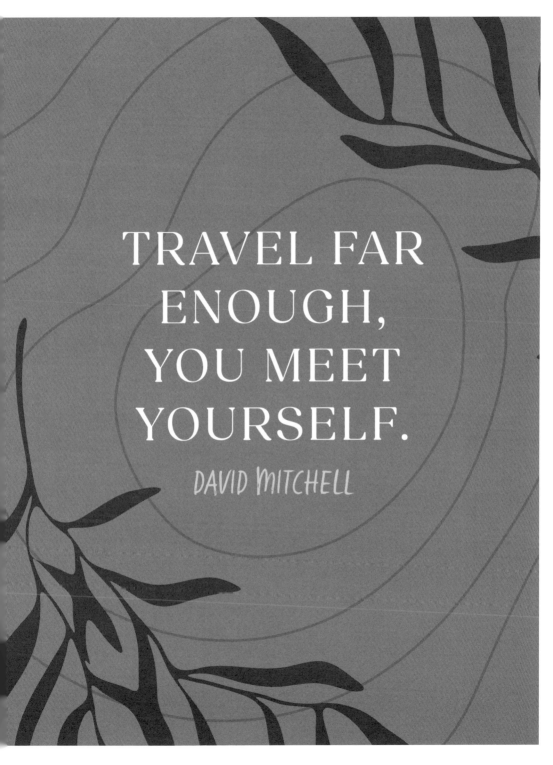

*Goals are dreams with deadlines.*

DIANA SCHARF

*Which projects do I want to complete this year?*

- 
- 
- 
- 
- 
- 
- 
- 
- 
- 
- 
-

*To whom will I write letters?*

- 
- 
- 
- 
- 
- 
- 
- 
- 
- 
- 
-

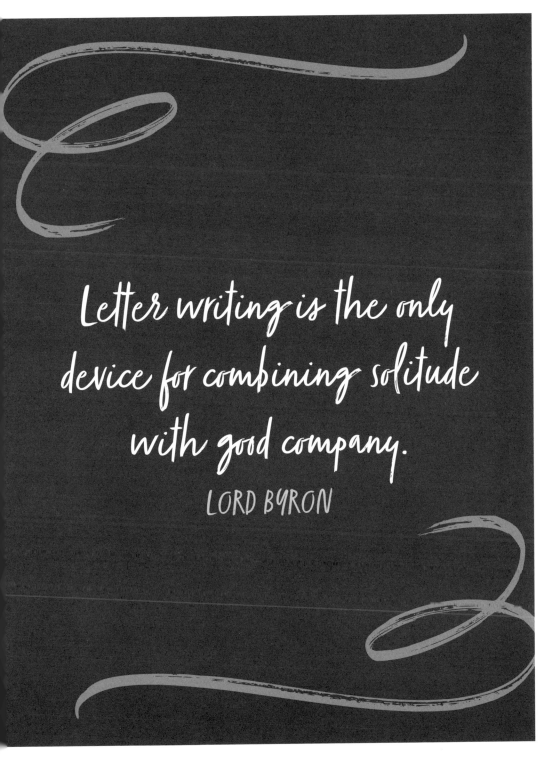

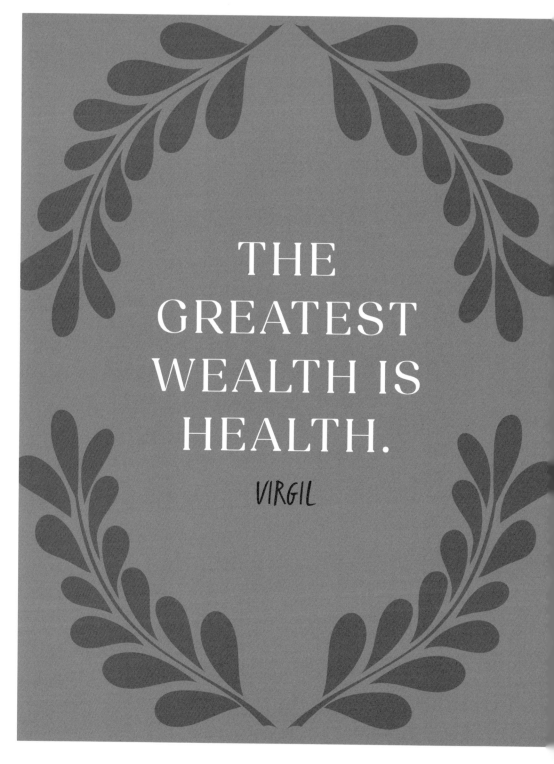

*What will I do to protect my health this year?*

- 
- 
- 
- 
- 
- 
- 
- 
- 
- 
- 
-

*Which habits do I want to cultivate?*

- 
- 
- 
- 
- 
- 
- 
- 
- 
- 
- 
-

# WHAT WE DO NOW ECHOES IN ETERNITY.

## MARCUS AURELIUS